"*I am very happy to endorse this devotional book. Melton has skillfully woven together spiritual insights, psychological understandings, scriptural interpretation, and self-care practices to create an incredibly moving and helpful resource. It is clearly directed towards African American women, but I can't imagine there is anyone who would not benefit from following these devotions, prayers, and self-care practices. I hope people will read it, follow it, repeat it, and pass it on to others.*"

-Dr. James P. Ashmore, former Assistant Dean and Associate Professor of Old Testament, Shaw University Divinity School

"*As a theologically trained and wise therapist who cares deeply about the experiences of Black women, Melanie Melton reminds readers of some very important truths: you are made in God's image and you matter. Your worth is not in what you produce, but in who you are. You are worthy of respect. You can carry your suffering to God and others, so that they can carry you. These are truths that everyone in our stressed, trauma-filled culture needs to hear.*"

–Warren Kinghorn, MD, ThD, Duke Divinity School

Queen, Let's Heal

QUEEN, LET'S HEAL:

Seven Day Devotional for Black Women

Melanie Melton, MA, LMFT, ThM, M.Div

Queen, Let's Heal
Seven Day Devotional for Black Women

Copyright © 2022 Now, Healing Begins, PLLC

All Rights Reserved.

No part of this book may be used or reproduced in any manner whatsoever without the prior permission except in the case of brief quotations embodied in critical articles or reviews.

Unless otherwise indicated, all Scripture quotations are taken from the *Holy Bible*, New Living Translation, copyright © 1996, 2004, 2015 by Tyndale House Foundation. Used by permission of Tyndale House Publishers, Carol Stream, Illinois 60188. All rights reserved.

At the time of publication all web sites referenced in this book were valid. However, due to the fluid nature of the internet some addresses may have changes or the content may no longer be relevant.

The author has made every effort to trace the ownership of all quotes. In the event of a question arising from the use of a quote, we regret any error made and will be pleased to make the necessary correction in future printing and editions of this book.

Limit of Liability/Disclaimer of Warranty

While the author has used their best efforts in preparing this document, they make no representation or warranties with respect to the accuracy or completeness of the contents and specifically disclaim any implied warranties. The information and strategies contained herein are not clinical nor ministerial recommendations and may not be suitable for your situation. It is strongly recommended that you consult with a licensed professional, where appropriate. The author shall not be liable for any loss or profit or any other commercial damages, including but not limited to special, incidental, consequential, relational or other damages.

Cover design: Rebecacovers

Images used under license from Adobe.com

Cover art: Adobe/pikselstock, 505892215-stock.adobe.com. Beautiful young woman enjoying spring in the park.

Interior Images art:

Adobe/atthameeni, 499781737-stock.adobe.com. wisdom line icon.

Adobe/- Bitter -, 188878696-stock.adobe.com. Bible, Scripture logo or label. Faith, creed, prayer icon.

Adobe/ali, 417171839-stock.adobe.com. Afro Woman, Black Girl, African American Woman, Strong Woman, Curly Hair, Afro Queen.

Printed in the U.S.A.

First Edition: 2022

This devotional is dedicated to my Matriarch, Mama Dear, who taught me to love Christ, love myself, and love others well.

Table of Contents

Acknowledgments 1

Introduction 2

Sacred Pause One: Abide 6

Sacred Pause Two: Enough 11

Sacred Pause Three: Chosen 16

Sacred Pause Four: Rest, Please 21

Sacred Pause Five: Cry Together, Heal Together 26

Sacred Pause Six: Promised, Regardless 31

Sacred Pause Seven: The Queen in Me 36

Resources to Continue Your Healing Journey 40

Bibliography 42

About the Author 43

Book Melanie Melton to Educate 44

Acknowledgments

I surely do not enter and engage in this research, which produced this devotional, on my own. I must specifically acknowledge my mother Carol, father Kenneth, and sister Amber who are my forever cheerleaders and have taught much that impacts my view on life, Jesus, and healing today. I also acknowledge my grandmothers Gertie and Carolyn, who left a legacy and pathed the way for me to have such an opportunity to write, research, and publish to help fellow black women.

I must also thank my dearest SisterFriends, who mindfully listened and learned all about womanist theology, theologies in America, and mental health, which gave me space to do the integration work, even if they weren't so interested.

I also acknowledge Bishop Benjamin W. Mittman Sr., for encouraging me to unashamedly be myself, integrated spiritual gifts, and all.

Also, I acknowledge my Shaw University Divinity School professors, Dr. Ashmore, Dr. Bryan, Dr. Broadway and Dr. Kirk-Duggan, who first introduced me to womanist theology and womanist theologians. They also championed and mentored me in how to healthily integrate spiritual well-being and mental health. In a similar fashion, I acknowledge Dr. A.L. Hall, Dr. Kinghorn, and Dr. W. Wilson, my Duke Divinity School professors who created space, resources, and guidance to continue to grow in my area of research.

Lastly, I acknowledge the womanist theologians that began and planted good seed in the ground for this important work, my fellow womanists that teach me daily, and for the future womanists whom I hope to add on to the foundation for them to build upon.

Introduction

This devotional was designed, created, and prayed over in prayer just for you! It was created for the unique, beautiful, bold, amazing woman that you are in this present moment. It presents as a welcoming invitation. An invitation to spend sacred time with Jesus, as you are ushered into God's truths about you while lies you have been taught are kicked to the curb. This provides an invitation to grow into an even more healthy, whole, and healed version of yourself.

The foundation of this devotional derives from an article by Dr. Delores S. Williams titled, *Black Women's Surrogacy Experience and the Christian Notion of Redemption*[1]. Within this article, Williams speaks many truths which include a beckoning to fellow Black women to no longer accept the role of suffering by way of surrogacy, in choosing to take care of everyone around you and neglecting yourself, taking on every task instead of delegating, and accepting any form of abuse or treatment which you do not deserve. Within this devotional are also references to the books by Dr. Emilie M. Townes, *Breaking the Fine Rain of Death* along with *Christ on the Psych Ward* by David Finnegan-Hosey[2,3]. With significance to this devotional, Townes raises the importance of communal lamenting, and how vital it is to lament together. As you will note later in the devotional, this devotional is in itself an act of communal lamenting. Finnegan-Hosey addresses mental

---

[1] Delores Williams, "Black Women's Surrogacy Experience and the Christian Notion of Redemption," from Marit Trelstad [ed.], *Cross Examinations: Reflections on the Meaning of the Cross Today* (Augsburg Fortress, 2006), pp. 19-32

[2] Emilie Townes, *Breaking the Fine Rain of Death: African-American Health Issues and a Womanist Ethic of Care* (Continuum, 1998)

[3] David Finnegan-Hosey, *Christ on the Psych Ward* (Church Publishing, 2018)

illness while being a Christian, which is necessary to state not being in conflict, as we address past trauma, pain, suffering, and usher into healing through this journey.

How to use this devotional

The structure of this devotional is set up with seven Sacred Pauses. You may choose to sit with each Sacred Pause for one week or for one day-that is up to you and God. I encourage you to revisit this devotional over time. My prayer is that you engage with the scripture, the short lesson, and enjoy your personal prayer and revelation from the Most High God. You will also find a mental health note within each Sacred Pause. This is essential, as Finnegan-Hosey helps one to understand that you can love Jesus and still have struggles with your mental health[4]. In particular with this devotional's focus on healing from historical, intergenerational, and personal trauma that Williams speaks of using the term surrogacy, it can be clearly articulated that trauma can lead to mental illness or mental health struggles, thus making the mental health notes provided necessary.

This is a safe space where you can embrace your journey, pains, mental illnesses, and seek pathways for healing in Jesus. *As a warning*: if you have experienced sexual abuse or violence, Sacred Pause Three may be triggering—feel free to skip over this Sacred Pause or consider spending additional time as you allow the Lord to minister to you through this section.

If you allow it through this journey, healing and being more well will come. You, woman of God, are worthy.

This book does not constitute as nor is a substitute for mental health services nor considered advice..

---

[4] Finnegan-Hosey

Here then, is the opening prayer. Feel free to pray this prayer or offer a prayer of your own:

Lord, thank you for being God, apart from you there is no other. Thank you for loving me. Throughout this devotional, Lord please bring me into deeper awareness of your love for me. Help me Lord, to learn the truth about myself and release the lies the world has taught me. Help me Lord, to know I have permission from you and to therefore grow more in love with myself, and take better care of myself. Lord, please help me to discern the best mental health professionals to support me through this healing journey, as I know all genuine help comes from you. Thank you for being so caring, kind, and gracious towards me. I trust you and know you are with me in this journey. In Jesus' name, Amen.

Sacred Pause One: Abide

Sacred Pause One: Abide
John 15:9 NLT

As you begin this journey of spending more time with Jesus and embracing your healing in him, it is critical to intentionally let go of distractions in your mind, heart, and surroundings for this one moment.

 Reflect on this scripture in a quiet space:

Jesus said: **"I have loved you even as the Father has loved me. Remain in my love"**. John 15:9

As you receive these words from Jesus, allow them to help you remember that you are loved. The words also offer for you to resume or continue spending time in nurturing your relationship with Christ. God desires for you to experience unconditional love, every minute of every day. *How?* Simply by talking, writing, and thinking of the Lord, reading the Holy Bible and reflecting on your reading throughout each day, telling the Lord thank you, and asking God for help- "living life" with Jesus. Regardless of your life experiences and those whose love did not last or was a fake "love", Sis, you are loved totally and completely by the Lord. No, God's love never fades, waivers, nor changes.

During this time of reflection on this scripture, take a few deep breaths. Please, inhale as you think on and embrace a word and then exhale and release a word (listed below):

Inhale God's Love…(count of three)…Exhale Fear
Inhale God's Love…(count of three)…Exhale Fear
Inhale God's Love…(count of three)…Exhale Fear

Spend a few moments quietly sitting and reflecting on God's love and unconditional acceptance, and when you are ready, speak to God in prayer.

Prayer

*Mental health note: As you begin this healing journey with Jesus which includes naming past trauma and current struggles, it's important to speak a truth offered by David Finnegan-Hosey, which is that mental health struggles are not caused by faith issues or sin[5]. We experience mental health problems and trauma because we are human and humans that are invited by the Lord to remain in the Lord's love. God has loved you before you were born, so in the midst of the suffering, consider receiving the truth: You are Forever Loved by God.

---

[5] Finnegan-Hosey, 44

Sacred Pause One Reflection: Abide

Jesus said: "I have loved you even as the Father has loved me. Remain in my love". John 15:9

I am Forever Loved by God

Sacred Pause One Reflection: Abide

Jesus said: "I have loved you even as the Father has loved me. Remain in my love". John 15:9

_____

I am Forever Loved by God

Sacred Pause Two: Enough

Sacred Pause Two: Enough
Psalm 23:1 NLT

Within the foundational article by Dr. Delores S. Williams, she educates on a Black woman trope that originated during Black women's time of enslavement in America, the Mammy. Mammy was the woman that cared for her slave master's children, the slave master's family, and the inside of the home. Mammy is what we refer to today as the Strong Black Woman, who spends all of her time caring for the world while neglecting herself[6].

You can look at scripture and find a familiar reference point in Luke 10:38-42. Within this passage, Jesus visits sisters Mary and Martha. Mary sat at the feet of Jesus listening as he taught, while Martha was busy preparing the home in having the Messiah as their guest. While Martha was doing what seemed to be the best thing, being the Strong Black Woman caring for Jesus, let us glean Jesus' response in verses 41-42: "But the Lord said to her, "My dear Martha, you are worried and upset over all these details. There is only one thing worth being concerned about. Mary has discovered it, and it will not be taken away from her".

Allow yourself to absorb these words from Jesus which give you permission to stop using your time emptying yourself for others, and instead to rest in and learn from Jesus. It is your call to put down your superwoman cape.

---

[6] Williams, 20-22

Reflect on this scripture in a quiet space:

"The Lord is my shepherd; I have all that I need". Psalm 23:1

As you receive these words, allow them to remind you that you have all that you need. Allow them to remind you that you are enough. Many of us women overextend in the name of filling our own voids or esteem--yet, right where you sit today: you have all that you need. Another truth: those you care for, as you allow them to follow Jesus, have all that they need as well.

During this time of reflection on this scripture, take a few slow deep breaths. As you take these deep breaths, imagine taking off the superwoman cape and tossing it into the sea to never be recovered. Imagine feeling much lighter, with a smile on your face, as you worship the Lord.

Now, spend a few moments quietly sitting and reflecting on God's unconditional acceptance and provision for your life and those that you love. When you are ready, end this devotion time in prayer.

 Prayer

*Mental health note: David Finnegan-Hosey in his book, speaks of the notion of Enough, of Grace. I offer that perhaps, as you struggle, that you can rest in God's grace that is extended to you each day[7]. Perhaps, remembering that God's grace is sufficient can help you to know that you have permission to glean that without your superwoman cape...you are Enough.

---

[7] Finnegan-Hosey, 67

Sacred Pause Two Reflection: Enough

"The Lord is my shepherd; I have all that I need".
Psalm 23:1

_____
_____
_____
_____
_____
_____
_____
_____
_____
_____
_____
_____
_____
_____
_____

I am Enough

Sacred Pause Two Reflection: Enough

"The Lord is my shepherd; I have all that I need".
Psalm 23:1

_____
_____
_____
_____
_____
_____
_____
_____
_____
_____
_____
_____
_____
_____
_____
_____

I am Enough

Sacred Pause Three: Chosen

trigger reminder-content references sexual violence-feel free to skip

Sacred Pause Three: Chosen
Trigger Reminder-feel free to skip
Ephesians 1:4-5 NLT

Now, take a look at Esther Chapter 1 verses 10-13, highlighting verse 12: "On the seventh day of the feast, when King Xerxes was in high spirits because of the wine, he told the seven eunuchs who attended him—Mehuman, Biztha, Harbona, Bigtha, Abagtha, Zethar, and Carcas— 11 to bring Queen Vashti to him with the royal crown on her head. He wanted the nobles and all the other men to gaze on her beauty, for she was a very beautiful woman. 12 But when they conveyed the king's order to Queen Vashti, she refused to come. This made the king furious, and he burned with anger". In this passage, you can glean that the King wanted his wife to attend a party with fellow inebriated men, with her crown on her head- which some argue was to wear her crown-only. In this moment, the queen essentially gave up her crown and risked her life as she gave a "holy NO" to being sexually objectified.

This holy NO falls in line with a concept from Dr. Delores S. Williams, of Black women being forced to have sexual activity with their slave master and at times his wife and others. While you may have endured such violence yourself at no choice of your own, Williams is agreeing with Queen Vashti saying, NO!, to it being allowed or approved for Black women to endure such violence[8]. As Finnegan-Hosey offers, we were not created by God to suffer[9].

---

[8] Williams, 20-22; 30-31
[9] Finnegan-Hosey, 44

Allow this to usher you into an even deeper space with the Lord, to lament the violence you may have endured but to also remember that no matter what the world has taught, you are priceless.

 Reflect on this scripture in a quiet space:

"Even before he made the world, God loved us and chose us in Christ to be holy and without fault in his eyes". Ephesians 1:4-5

During this time of reflection on this scripture, take a few slow deep breaths:

Inhale Love…(count of three)… Exhale Pain

Inhale Acceptance…(count of three)… Exhale Rejection

Inhale Peace…(count of three)…Exhale Fear

Inhale Love…(count of three)…Exhale with praises unto God

Now, spend a few moments quietly sitting and reflecting on being chosen by God and God's love and care for you-even in the midst of violence that you may have endured. Honor all of the emotions that may arise and share them with God in prayer-the Lord can handle it and wants to help you. When you are ready, end this devotion time in prayer.

Prayer

*Mental health note: Sexual violence can cause much confusion around sex, identity, love, and so forth. You have begun this healing journey-be proud of yourself! Please also seek help, today, from a mental health professional to continue this healing journey. Resources are listed at the end of this devotional. You did NOT deserve the violence. You did NOT deserve the abuse. You absolutely DO deserve healing! You absolutely ARE loved and priceless! You ARE chosen by God!

Sacred Pause Three Reflection: Chosen

"Even before he made the world, God loved us and chose us in Christ to be holy and without fault in his eyes". Ephesians 1:4-5

_____
_____
_____
_____
_____
_____
_____
_____
_____
_____
_____
_____
_____
_____
_____

I AM absolutely loved and priceless!

Sacred Pause Three Reflection: Chosen

"Even before he made the world, God loved us and chose us in Christ to be holy and without fault in his eyes". Ephesians 1:4-5

I AM absolutely loved and priceless!

Sacred Pause Four: Rest, Please

Sacred Pause Four: Rest, Please
Mark 6:31 NLT

In the article by Dr. Delores S. Williams, she informs of Black women having to do field labor including tasks that were suited for male bodies. Williams pushes back against women today, signing up to overwork themselves or be enlisted to overdo it. Similarly to women wearing (now thrown away) superwoman capes, due to this history, Black women can accept the too many and too heavy tasks put on oneself[10].

Instead, I invite you to complete the tasks that God has assigned to you for each day-only. Then, consider following the model of Jesus and rest.

 Reflect on this scripture in a quiet space:

"Then Jesus said, 'Let's go off by ourselves to a quiet place and rest awhile'". Mark 6:31

If Jesus took the time to rest, give yourself permission to begin mandating your own rest as well. You need it. You deserve it. The work will get done without you, if you teach others that you will not always step in and do their part. It will all get done.

During this time of reflection on this scripture, take a few slow deep breaths. As you take these deep breaths, imagine yourself in your favorite restful location. As you imagine yourself in this space, whether it's your bed, the park, beach or another destination, imagine you laying down.

---

[10] Williams, 20-22; 30-31

Allow your body to relax and notice your safe surroundings. As you take in this peaceful scenery, speak these words to yourself: *I am Enough, I deserve Rest, I am resting just like Jesus.*

Now, spend a few moments quietly sitting and enjoying rest. Begin to imagine where in each day you can create time to rest and what tasks you can allow others to do for themselves. When you are ready, end this devotion time in prayer.

Prayer

***Mental health note:** Oftentimes, enduring trauma can make it scary for one to stop, to pause, in fear that all of the pain will overwhelm them. As you begin to allow yourself to rest, consider taking short breaks and lengthen them overtime. I also invite you to decide how to define healthy rest for you: that may mean taking a walk, a nap, doing a crossword puzzle, coloring book, or looking at nature--feel free to define what is most healthy and restful for each day.

Sacred Pause Four Reflection: Rest, Please

"Then Jesus said, 'Let's go off by ourselves to a quiet place and rest awhile'". Mark 6:31

I am Enough, I deserve Rest

Sacred Pause Four Reflection: Rest, Please

"Then Jesus said, 'Let's go off by ourselves to a quiet place and rest awhile'". Mark 6:31

_____
_____
_____
_____
_____
_____
_____
_____
_____
_____
_____
_____
_____
_____
_____
_____
_____

I am Enough, I deserve Rest

Sacred Pause Five: Cry Together, Heal Together

Sacred Pause Five:
Cry Together, Heal Together
2 Corinthians 1:4 NLT

Dr. Emilie M. Townes, in her book, *Breaking the Fine Rain of Death*, teaches about the importance of communal lamenting. She describes, "a corporate experience of calling for healing, makes suffering bearable and manageable in the community"[11]. Townes also shares that rather than trying to ignore the experience or appear strong, that in choosing to lament and grieve, we are simultaneously acknowledging our experience[12]. You, Sis, have spent time through this devotional operating in communal lament with the Lord, by naming past trauma, lies from society, and seeking wellness as you have spent more time with Jesus!

Yes, sis, you have been doing this healing work with Jesus! Every moment is a great moment for a Praise Break!!! You have put down the superwoman cape, are working on reclaiming your complete love and value in Christ and are allowing yourself to Rest. Now, please exhale the tears that you have been crying on the inside. God hears your tears, and cares.

 Reflect on this scripture in a quiet space:

"He comforts us in all our troubles so that we can comfort others. When they are troubled, we will be able to give them the same comfort God has given us". 2 Corinthians 1:4

---

[11] Townes, 24
[12] Townes, 24

Your tears matter. Every single one. Not only that, but God is also with you and comforts you with every tear you cry, even as you hold your tears on the inside. As you keep going in this healing work with Jesus, it is essential that you release the pain and make room for God's healing.

During this time of reflection on this scripture, take a few slow deep breaths.

Inhale Joy…(count of three)…Exhale Pain
Inhale Peace…(count of three)…Exhale Chaos
Inhale Love…(count of three)…Exhale Trauma, Pain

Spend a few moments quietly sitting and thinking on how if for you, communal lament also means calling on a trusted friend, so you can comfort and support one another. We all suffer. We do not have to suffer nor heal in silence. When you are ready, end this devotion time in prayer.

 Prayer

*Mental health note: David Finnegan-Hosey shares that church congregations in the United States tend to avoid lamenting[13]. Therefore, you may find it challenging to talk with those in your church about the deep pains-that is okay. Lamenting is hard work; it is also a skill. As you learn this necessary skill, seek safe places today for support, whether it's family, friends, church members, a support group, or therapy. You can locate resources provided at the end of this devotional and contact them today.

---

[13] Finnegan-Hosey, 42

Sacred Pause Five Reflection: Cry Together, Heal Together

"He comforts us in all our troubles so that we can comfort others. When they are troubled, we will be able to give them the same comfort God has given us". 2 Corinthians 1:4

_____
_____
_____
_____
_____
_____
_____
_____
_____
_____
_____
_____
_____
_____
_____

I am Inhaling Joy...(count of three)...and Exhaling Pain

Sacred Pause Five Reflection: Cry Together, Heal Together

"He comforts us in all our troubles so that we can comfort others. When they are troubled, we will be able to give them the same comfort God has given us". 2 Corinthians 1:4

_____
_____
_____
_____
_____
_____
_____
_____
_____
_____
_____
_____
_____
_____
_____
_____

I am Inhaling Joy...(count of three)...and Exhaling Pain

Sacred Pause Six: Promised, Regardless

Sacred Pause Six: Promised, Regardless
Genesis 21:1 NLT

Take a look at Genesis 21:1, **"The Lord kept his word and did for Sarah exactly what he had promised"**. What came before this passage was God promising a son and inheritance to Sarah and Abraham, Sarah and Abraham lying about being married twice-even causing other women to become infertile, and Sarah mandating Hagar to birth Ishmael in an attempt to make God's promise happen. Essentially, we watched many fails from Sarah (and Abraham). Yet this verse and following verses inform that God kept the original promise to Sarah.

As you have spent time throughout this devotional, many emotions may have arisen along with many memories. While the article by Dr. Delores S. Williams was absolutely debunking Black women being surrogates in the forms of taking care of the world, outsourcing their bodies to others, and over working to one's own neglect---it was not placing shame nor blame on Black women. Rather, she shared these roles being birthed from Black women's history, not by choice. However, she is now extending the choice to demolish these unhealthy roles in your hands, by following healthy models in the Bible[14]. The promises of God for your life are not contingent on you maintaining these unhealthy roles nor living a "perfect" life (which is impossible, Sis).

This offers you an opportunity to recognize where you may carry out unhealthy roles in your life and work towards being healthier and with the understanding that scripture approves of you doing so. The promises do not change if you never pick up that superwoman cape

---

[14] Williams, 23-27, 30-31

again! Even if others are not happy with this healthier you-the promises of God still stand.

 Reflect on this scripture in a quiet space:

"The Lord kept his word and did for Sarah exactly what he had promised". Genesis 21:1

During this time of reflection on this scripture, take a few slow deep breaths. As you take these breaths, remember the promises that God has spoken over your life, like that you are always loved and chosen by God. Allow yourself to smile as you remember all of God's promises, knowing that you have to do nothing to earn them or force them to happen. You are loved and kept by God, who loved you before you loved him. There is hope and permission for a healthier life in Christ.

Now, spend a few moments quietly sitting and reflecting on God's promises for your life. Spend a few moments writing them down as reminders of hope on the hard days. Regardless of what you have endured or the too many capes you wear, God's promises still reign true. When you are ready, end this devotion time in prayer.

Prayer

*Mental health note: As you begin to dream and believe again about all that God has promised you it is important to say out loud: My Trauma, My Pain, My mental health struggles have not caused my "delay"! You are not responsible for your trauma, nor any abuse you have received, pain you have endured due to suffering, nor mental health struggles. God's love for you is complete, you are complete, and the Lord's promises will reign. God's timing is something you cannot fully understand beforehand, but you can rest in these truths.

Sacred Pause Six Reflection: Promised, Regardless

"The Lord kept his word and did for Sarah exactly what he had promised". Genesis 21:1

_____
_____
_____
_____
_____
_____
_____
_____
_____
_____
_____
_____
_____
_____
_____
_____
_____
_____

My Trauma, My Pain, My mental health struggles have not caused my "delay"!

Sacred Pause Six Reflection: Promised, Regardless

"The Lord kept his word and did for Sarah exactly what he had promised". Genesis 21:1

___

My Trauma, My Pain, My mental health struggles have not caused my "delay"!

Sacred Pause Seven: The Queen in Me

Sacred Pause Seven: The Queen in Me
Psalm 139:14 NLT

Enough, Chosen, Loved, Deserving of Rest, Promised-Regardless, with Every Tear counting--those are the truths about You! This journey with the help of the authors have assisted in naming where some of your trauma, mental health struggles, and pain come from. As vital as it is to name your pains and their origins, this journey was created to allow you to create space to tell yourself the TRUTH! While our society may still try to put you in a role of suffering, or surrogacy for the greater good-you are worth so much more and made for so much more! While you will go through mountain highs and valley lows with your complexity and all, you, Black woman, were not made by God for the sole purpose of suffering. Of many things, you were created already Loved and to learn to Love others well, with the Love of Christ, which means you must first learn to Love yourself Well.

Scripture can help you remember this truth: "**So God created human beings in his own image**". **Genesis 1:27A**

God! Divinity, Perfection, Creator, Liberator, Healer! God created You in his own image! Flaws, pain, trauma-complex you: you were made in the image of the Divine! It is genuinely past time for us to kick to the curb all of the lies of the enemy, society, and even that you have told yourself and instead, receive who God says you are! This is not a one-time task but a "to-do" every single day.

Reflect on this scripture in a quiet space:

"Thank you for making me so wonderfully complex! Your workmanship is marvelous—how well I know it". Psalm 139:14

During this time of reflection on this scripture, take a few slow deep breaths. As you take these deep breaths, imagine looking at yourself in the mirror (or actually look at yourself in the mirror!), noting all of your beauty, all of the things that make you complex and oh so marvelous!

Now, spend a few moments praising the Lord for making you in his image and so marvelous and complex--through it all! When you are ready, end this devotion time in prayer.

 Prayer

***Mental health note:** I am tremendously grateful that God has begun you on this journey of healing from trauma, pain, suffering. Please remember to take it one step at a time, and that your journey is yours and different than anyone else's. Please do contact a therapist today and allow them to help you continue the journey (information on next page). Please always use any of the crisis services listed for additional mental health support. You are here because of God's unconditional love for you. As you keep walking, know you are loved, seen, valued, validated, and supported!

Sacred Pause Seven Reflection: The Queen in Me

"Thank you for making me so wonderfully complex! Your workmanship is marvelous—how well I know it". Psalm 139:14

_____
_____
_____
_____
_____
_____
_____
_____
_____
_____
_____
_____
_____
_____
_____
_____
_____
_____
_____

Enough, Chosen, Loved, Deserving of Rest, Promised-Regardless, with Every Tear counting--those are the truths about Me!

Sacred Pause Seven Reflection: The Queen in Me

"Thank you for making me so wonderfully complex! Your workmanship is marvelous—how well I know it". Psalm 139:14

_____
_____
_____
_____
_____
_____
_____
_____
_____
_____
_____
_____
_____
_____
_____
_____

Enough, Chosen, Loved, Deserving of Rest, Promised-Regardless, with Every Tear counting--those are the truths about Me!

Resources to Continue Your Healing Journey

Sis, you have worked so hard to allow Jesus to heal you through this devotional. Please keep it going and seek a local or virtual therapist! You deserve it!

This is not an endorsement of the services from the resources shared and the author is not liable for care services rendered by resources listed.

Therapists:
Therapy for Black Girls:
https://providers.therapyforblackgirls.com/

Black Female Therapists:
https://www.blackfemaletherapists.com/

Crisis Services:
Crisis Text Line
Text HOME to 741741 to reach a volunteer Crisis Counselor
https://www.crisistextline.org/

National Suicide Prevention Lifeline
Dial 988
24 hours/7 days per wk
www.suicidepreventionlifeline.org

National Hopeline Network/IMAlive
1-800-SUICIDE
24 hours/7 days per wk
www.hopeline.com
1-800-784-2433

Online Resources:

    RAINN for sexual assault survivors

    https://www.rainn.org/consulting-services#hotline

National Suicide Hotlines

    http://www.suicidehotlines.com

National Suicide Prevention Resource Center

    http://www.sprc.org

Substance Abuse and Mental Health Services Administration

    https://www.samhsa.gov/

Bibliography

Williams, Delores S. "Black Women's Surrogacy Experience and the Christian Notion of Redemption," from Marit Trelstad [ed.], *Cross Examinations: Reflections on the Meaning of the Cross Today* (Augsburg Fortress, 2006), pp. 19-32

Townes, Emilie. *Breaking the Fine Rain of Death: African-American Health Issues and a Womanist Ethic of Care* (Continuum, 1998)

Finnegan-Hosey, David. *Christ on the Psych Ward* (Church Publishing, 2018)

About the Author

Melanie Melton, MA, LMFT, ThM, M.Div

Ms. Melton, a native of Texas, holds a Bachelor of Science degree in Family Community Services from East Carolina University and Master of Marriage Family Therapy degree from Appalachian State University. She also earned her Master of Divinity degree from Shaw University Divinity School and Master of Theology degree from Duke Divinity School.

Ms. Melton's research focuses on black women, theology's impact on black women's mental health, and pathways toward healing. She intentionally engages her research through the integration of mental health, mental illness, womanist theology, and spiritual well-being.

Ms. Melton is a North Carolina Licensed Marriage and Family Therapist and Ordained Minister. She holds certifications and provides trauma-informed therapy, including EMDR and Trauma Focused Cognitive Behavioral Therapy. Ms. Melton is the Founder and Owner of Now, Healing Begins, PLLC, which seeks to offer services to the African American community, including to address mental and spiritual well-being (nowhealingbegins.com).

Not only does Ms. Melton bring much depth of clinical and ministry related experience to her work, but she also brings her compassionate and mindful lens in having loved ones with mental illness and mental health struggles. Ms. Melton is an educator and proponent of being mentally and spiritually well, and also intentionally engages in self-care, including quality time with loved ones, time in nature, enjoying music, and watching Dallas Cowboys and ECU Pirates Football!

Book Melanie Melton to Educate

Melanie is available for book signings, speaking engagements, workshops, and consultation.

For more information and to book Melanie for your next event, visit www.nowhealingbegins.com or connect at info@nowhealingbegins.

Made in the USA
Columbia, SC
17 June 2023

18202554R00028